As

Thinketh:

21 Keys To Avoid Thinking Mediocre, Low Value, And Basic.

Introduction

I honestly feel like this book was a gift from God, through divine inspiration and motivation, filled with truths, wisdom, and profound literature that God urged me to read. I know that God will lead us to information and teachings needed to grow into the person

He called us to be. It's on us to accept that God has a purpose for us and to trust the process of His guidance. We are groomed through education in truth and proper knowledge, which lifts us out of darkness by illuminating our minds.

In the earlier parts of my life, I was a completely different person. The man who wrote this book is surely a product of God's work. My concept of what was 'real' and what being a 'Real One' was, was a very warped concept. I thought that being prone to mischief, ready to commit acts of violence, okay with engaging in criminal activity, aligned with the underworld and other 'low vibrational' people, and being a fan favorite of different women that I didn't see true value in was being a 'Real One.' All along, I had bought into illusions and couldn't see what was real at all. The way of thinking that I had kept me impoverished spiritually and physically and eventually led me to prison.

It was in prison that God transformed me spiritually and mentally. My heart and mind had to be pried open. While God was working on my spirit, He also illuminated my mind by introducing me to esoteric literature, scriptures, and many other profound writings

concealed within books. After starting to think differently and moving with a renewed spirit, I learned that my entire being had changed through God and education. Through both, I became anew. By way of both, God and education freed me from a 40-year sentence

after spending over a decade incarcerated. I found myself married to the woman of my dreams and having more material wealth than I ever imagined. I did the inner work, and God played a crucial role.

It was a must to credit God and education for life change. The change of mind and cleansing of spirit that I got to experience and experience daily is the change that I wanted others to experience. The growth and development that I gained were the growth and development I wanted others to gain. I wanted to see others get free from mental and spiritual bondage. I understood that a relationship with God and education is the key to that liberation. I compiled a small amount of knowledge and wisdom that I was imparted with by God or was inspired to deliver during my own studying of profound esoteric literature, the Bible, the Quran, and other spiritual and intellectual foods. I prayed that God would order my steps and move me to include some of my writings in this book to be a resource for the expansion of the mind strengthening of the spirit, and the relationship with God. I've oversimplified my process in life to save from writing an autobiography. However, I have shared some Divinely inspired knowledge, wisdom, and perspective for the seekers of truth, enlightenment, and peace.

Better equipment produces better results. Build yourself so that you can be a valuable tool for God to use.

Zay Perry

December of '2023

Thanks & Dedications

I thank God for giving me the able body, mind, and willing spirit to prepare this book. I thank my fiancée Kea, who is beautiful in all of her being and is my gift from God. I thank my brother R.J., who never left me stranded during my harshest times. I thank anyone who added on to my growth and development positively. I thank my mother and father for being vessels to give me life. I thank my sister for care in my youth. I also want to give thanks to my close friends and brothers Maurice (Cheeks) and Vincent (Be Righteous) for loyalty, encouragement, and add ons.

This work is dedicated to:

The Most High God, My fiancée Kea, My daughters Khari & Journey, My unborn son, My brother John B.

TABLE OF CONTENTS

Quote By The Author

Every day, make sure to refresh your mental focus and maintain a heart filled with gratitude, accepting the best things destined for you. Your state of mind is the ultimate boundary of your life; ensure it is always primed for success, peace, and contentment.

If you persist in your old ways that have never yielded positive outcomes, then it is obvious that you are content with failure.

-Zay Perry

Key #1: The Power Of Thought: Shaping Your Destiny

Have you ever heard that saying, 'As a person thinks in their heart, so they are'? Let me tell you, it's not just words; it's the truth that shapes who we become. Your thoughts? They're the blueprint of your life, the seeds from which your actions grow, whether they sprout quickly or take time to unfold.

Your actions? They're the fruit of your thoughts. Think negatively, and pain is right there, following like a shadow. But reside in that realm of purity, and joy becomes your steadfast companion.

Listen closely, everyone: we aren't accidents. We're the sum of our ongoing thoughts. Having a noble character isn't luck; it's the result of consistently embracing higher thoughts. But delve into those base thoughts, and it shapes a different path.

The power is in our hands, friends. We're the architects of our own destinies, shaping our lives with the tools our thoughts create. Choose your thoughts wisely, and you elevate yourself. Misuse that power, and you are on a downward spiral.

But here's the deal: even in the toughest times, you're in charge. The key? Understanding your own thoughts, delving deep into your soul, and taking control of the 'household' within. It's about introspection, learning from experience, and applying that knowledge.

Life's a treasure trove of truths, waiting for us to dig deep. You're the sculptor of your life, the one who shapes your destiny. How? By observing, managing, and transforming your thoughts. This isn't just theory; it's a practical journey of self-discovery, connecting the dots between what you think, what you do, and what unfolds around you.

Remember, seeking wisdom takes time, practice, and relentless pursuit. Keep knocking; that door of understanding will swing wide open.

Your destiny? It's in your hands, everyone. Craft it with wisdom, seize it with power. You're the captain of your own ship.

Key #2: Balanced Existence

Calmness of mind, my brothers and sisters, is a precious gem of wisdom that shines brightly in our lives. It's not something that comes easy; it's a product of tireless dedication to mastering oneself. When you see someone who carries this calmness, it speaks volumes about their experience and their profound understanding of how thoughts shape our existence.

See, a person finds peace as they recognize themselves as beings born from thought. This understanding naturally extends to others, realizing they too are products of thought. As this awareness grows, the chaos of fretting, worrying, and grieving diminishes, leaving behind a poised and steady soul.

The serene individual, having learned self-mastery, knows how to relate to others with grace. People gravitate towards this spiritual strength, seeking to learn from and lean on them. The more tranquil a person becomes, the more their success and influence flourish. Even in everyday dealings, a person with steady equanimity attracts others.

That composed, strong soul is cherished and respected by many. They're like a refreshing oasis in a parched land or a sturdy shelter in a raging storm. Who wouldn't appreciate a heart at peace, a life well-balanced? Rain or shine, those who possess these gifts remain unruffled, calm, and serene. This serene character, this serenity we speak of, it's the ultimate product of refinement, a treasure surpassing even the value of gold.

Think about it, how many lives turn sour due to explosive tempers, destroying the beauty and sweetness within? Lack of self-control ruins happiness for many. But how rare it is to encounter those with a well-balanced, refined character, embodying that exquisite equilibrium.

In this world of turbulent emotions, only the wise, the ones who master their thoughts, can steer the storms of the soul. To those tossed by life's storms, wherever you are, remember this: amidst life's vast ocean, there are islands of happiness gleaming, and your ideal shore awaits your arrival. Keep a firm grip on the helm of your thoughts. Within your soul's vessel lies the commanding Master; He slumbers, waiting for your call. Self-control is strength, Right Thought is mastery, and Calmness is power. Say to your heart, "Peace, be still!"

Key #3: Wellbeing Through Mind Beautification

The influence of thoughts on health and the body is profound, my friend. You see, the body is akin to a devoted servant to the mind, heeding its commands, whether consciously chosen or expressed unknowingly. When our thoughts turn negative and troubled, the body follows suit, succumbing to illness and decline. But when we embrace joyful and beautiful thoughts, the body, ah, it blossoms with vitality and grace.

Let me tell you, illness and health—they find their roots in our thoughts. Negative thoughts, my friend, materialize in our bodies. Anxious thoughts? They can seize life faster than a bullet. They have a way of claiming lives, slowly but surely. Those who fear illness? They often find themselves affected. Anxiety? It undermines the body, making it susceptible to ailments. And impure thoughts? Even if left unacted upon, they can wreak havoc on the entire nervous system.

However, those resilient, pure, and joyful thoughts? They fortify the body—making it robust and poised. The body, my friend, is like an instrument, attuned to the thoughts we impress upon it. Our patterns of thought, they wield their own influence on it, for better or worse.

People will continue to have impure blood until they cleanse those thoughts, believe me. A pure heart? That begets a pure life and a pure body. But a disordered mind? It yields a chaotic life and a tainted body. Thought, my friend, is the genesis of action, life, and all that manifests. Purify that wellspring, and everything else falls into place.

Altering your diet won't suffice if you don't change your thoughts, friend. Once a person purifies their thoughts, impure cravings fade away.

Pure thoughts foster pure habits. And let me tell you, that supposed saint neglecting personal hygiene isn't a saint at all. Strengthen and purify your thoughts, and those harmful microbes won't trouble you.

Safeguard your mind if you wish to safeguard your body. Beautify your mind if you aim to rejuvenate your body. Negative thoughts of spite, envy, disappointment—they rob health and elegance from the body. A troubled countenance? It's not happenstance, my friend. It's sculpted by troubled thoughts. Wrinkles? They're etched by folly, passion, and pride.

Let me share something with you. I know a ninety-six-year-old individual with a visage as innocent and radiant as a young person's. Conversely, there's a man, not even middle-aged, yet his countenance reflects a life of discord. One is the result of a sunny disposition, the other born from passion and dissatisfaction.

Just as a home lacks sweetness and health without fresh air and sunlight, a strong body and a cheerful countenance necessitate joyful and tranquil thoughts flooding the mind.

Observe the faces of the elderly, my friend. There are wrinkles of compassion, carved by strong and pure thoughts, and then there are those etched by passion. Do you see the contrast? For those who've lived virtuously, age brings tranquility, like a setting sun. I recall this philosopher on his deathbed. Not old in years, but he departed this world as peacefully as he lived in it.

Positive thoughts, my friend, are akin to the finest medicine for bodily woes. And goodwill? There's no solace quite like it when shadows of grief and sorrow linger. But to dwell in a perpetual state of ill will, cynicism, suspicion, and envy? That's akin to being trapped in a self-fashioned prison. Now, thinking well of all, being cheerful, and earnestly seeking good in everyone—those selfless thoughts? They're the gates to a better place. And dwelling daily in thoughts of peace toward every being? That, my friend, brings boundless peace to the one who embraces them.

Key #4: Using Your Mind & Having Purpose

Until you connect your thoughts with a purpose, you won't achieve true intelligence. For many, thoughts aimlessly wander without direction on life's journey. Wandering aimlessly is a problem, and it is not the way to avoid disaster.

Those without a clear life purpose easily fall into worry, fear, troubles, and self-pity, showing signs of weakness. These lead to failure and unhappiness, just like planned sins, but through a different path. In a universe evolving with power, weakness can't stand.

A person should conceive a genuine purpose and pursue it wholeheartedly. It could be a spiritual ideal or a worldly goal but focus thoughts on it. Make it the central point. Don't let your mind wander into passing fancies or daydreams. This leads to self-control and real concentration. Even in failures, the character gained becomes the measure of true success, a steppingstone for future triumphs.

If someone isn't ready for a grand purpose, focus on doing their duty flawlessly, no matter how small it seems. This gathers thoughts, builds resolution, and generates energy. Then, nothing seems impossible.

The weakest soul, aware of its weakness, understands that strength develops through effort and practice. Believing this, they start working, adding effort upon effort, patience upon patience, and strength upon strength, never ceasing to grow stronger.

Like a physically weak person becomes strong through training, weak thoughts can become strong through right thinking.

Abandon aimlessness and weakness, start thinking purposefully, and join the league of the strong who see failure as a step towards success. They make conditions work for them, think boldly, act fearlessly, and achieve masterfully.

Once a purpose is conceived, mentally carve a straight path to achieve it, without distractions. Exclude doubts and fears; they disrupt efforts, making them ineffective. Doubt and fear achieve nothing but failure. Purpose, energy, and strong thoughts vanish when doubt and fear sneak in.

The will to act springs from knowing we can. Doubt and fear hinder knowledge and sabotage progress at every turn.

Conquer doubt and fear, and you conquer failure. Align every thought with power, facing difficulties bravely and overcoming them wisely. Plant your purposes thoughtfully, watch them bloom, and bear fruit that doesn't fall prematurely.

When thoughts merge fearlessly with purpose, they become creative energy. Knowing this transforms you into something more than just fleeting thoughts and sensations. It makes you the conscious wielder of your mental powers.

Key #5: Mind Matters: Achieving Goals

In life, everything an individual achieves or fails to achieve is directly connected to their thoughts. In a world requiring balance, personal responsibility is absolute. Weaknesses, strengths, purity, impurities—all self-made, not influenced by others. Changing these traits? That's on the individual, not others. Where one stands in life, that's their own doing, too. Joy and pain? Stem from within. Thinking shapes who someone is and who they'll become.

A strong individual can't uplift someone unwilling to be helped. Even if they are, the weaker person must find their strength, put in their own effort to attain what they admire in another. No one else can alter their circumstances.

Once it was said, "Many are enslaved because of one oppressor; let's hate the oppressor." Now, some think differently. They say, "One person oppresses because many are enslaved; let's have no respect for that enslavement."

Truth is, both oppressor and oppressed dwell in darkness. They harm each other but hurt themselves even more. True understanding perceives the law in the weakness of the oppressed and the misguided power of the oppressor. Real love doesn't blame either; it embraces both. One who's shed weakness and selfish thoughts? They don't belong to either side. They're free.

You can only rise by elevating your thoughts. Stuck in lowly thinking? You'll remain weak and miserable.

Before achieving anything, even in the world, an individual must rise above base desires. Not rid themselves entirely but let some go. Lost in animal desires? Can't think clearly, can't plan well, can't access hidden potential. If thoughts can't be controlled, serious matters can't be handled. Limits? Set by chosen thoughts.

No progress, no success without sacrifice. Worldly success tied to sacrificing chaotic animal thoughts. Focus on plans, strengthen resolve and self-reliance. Higher thoughts lead to betterment, more success, and enduring achievements.

The universe doesn't favor the greedy or dishonest, despite appearances. It backs the honest, big-hearted, virtuous. Great teachers conveyed this in various ways. To witness it? Elevate thoughts, become more virtuous.

Intellectual achievements born from thoughts seeking knowledge, truth, beauty—not vanity or ambition. Result of hard, selfless work.

Spiritual achievements? Summit of noble aspirations. Reside in high thoughts, focus on purity and selflessness, grow wise and noble. Rise to influence and blessedness as surely as the sun rises.

Achievement, in any form, is the result of effort and thought. Self-control, purity, righteousness, focused thoughts—ascend. Animality, laziness, impurity, corruption, muddled thinking—descend.

One might reach great heights but fall by succumbing to arrogance, selfishness, corruption.

Victories from right thinking need guarding. Many falter after winning, sliding into failure.

All achievements, in business, intellect, or spirit, follow the same law: directed thought. Goal differs, that's all.

To achieve little, give up a little. For much, sacrifice much. Immense sacrifices for great heights.

Key #6: Philosophies & Ambitions

In the grand scheme, dreamers serve as the world's rescuers. Just as the seen relies on the unseen, people draw sustenance from the profound dreams of solitary thinkers amid their trials and mundane routines. Humanity cannot abandon its dreamers; their ideals must not wither or perish. They are alive within us, destined to materialize as our future realities.

Originators—musicians, sculptors, artists, wordsmiths, seers, and wise individuals—shape the world beyond, crafting the very essence of heaven. Their existence renders this world beautiful; without them, humankind would falter.

Those who nurture magnificent visions, lofty ideals within, will one day bring them to fruition. Columbus dreamt of another world and uncovered it; Copernicus fostered the vision of a vast universe and multiple worlds, revealing it; Buddha beheld a realm of spiritual purity and serenity, entering it.

Embrace your visions, ideals, and the stirring melodies within your heart, the beauty taking shape in your mind. From these, all blissful conditions will emerge, creating a heavenly environment. Stay true to them, and your world will ultimately take form from these foundations.

Desire leads to attainment; aspiration leads to achievement. Shall base desires find fulfillment while noble aspirations deteriorate? No, such is not the law; this cannot persist. Ask, and you shall receive.

Dream ambitious dreams, for as you dream, so shall you become. Your vision foretells your future self; your ideal unveils your destiny.

Every great accomplishment begins as a dream. The oak lies dormant within the acorn; the bird awaits in the egg; within the soul's highest vision, an awakening angel stirs. Dreams sow the seeds of reality.

Your circumstances may seem adverse, but they won't linger if you grasp an ideal and strive towards it. You can't progress internally while remaining stagnant externally. Consider a youth burdened by poverty, toiling in an unhealthy workshop, lacking refinement. Yet, they dream of intelligence, refinement, grace, and beauty. They envision a life of freedom and broader horizons, driving them to action. They dedicate their time and meager resources to develop their latent abilities. Soon, their transformed mindset makes the workshop incompatible. With new opportunities aligned with their expanding potential, they leave it behind forever. Years later, they emerge as a person of profound influence, mastering the forces of the mind. Lives change at their words; they become a pivotal figure around whom countless destinies revolve. They have fulfilled their youthful vision, becoming one with their ideal.

And you, dear reader, will materialize the vision in your heart—whether base or beautiful, or a mix of both. You'll gravitate toward what you secretly love most. Your thoughts will yield exact results; you'll reap what you sow—no more, no less. Your current situation will shift with your thoughts, vision, and ideal. You'll shrink or soar according to your desires and aspirations.

In life, there are efforts and there are outcomes, and the vigor of the effort measures the result. Luck isn't a factor. Gifts, abilities, material, intellectual, and spiritual possessions—all fruits of endeavor—represent thoughts materialized, tasks completed, dreams realized.

The vision you honor in your mind, the ideal you enthrone in your heart—these will shape your life, define your becoming.

Key# 7 : Clearing A Space To Build And Make

Before a new way of thinking and a new way of life can be put in place, there must be the process of identifying what is already in place and needs to be done away with to make way for the new and better. We have to DO THE WORK, take the necessary time, and make a diligent effort to identify the problems and their sources. After identifying the problem, then we can alleviate or address its source, and thus, resolve the problem. Once we eliminate the problematic conditions, then we can put new things in our lives that create new circumstances that are beneficial to our community of Self and subsequently will be beneficial to the community that we are a part of.

An individual might ask himself or his particular group that he aligns himself with, "Why should I look to change my or our way of thinking and way of life?" A simple and most meaningful answer would be: "Because no individual is perfect, and hardly ever is any situation readily perfect, so we need to mold ourselves into individuals who create and maintain fulfilling and peaceful lives, and also create and maintain conditions and communities that are peaceful and fulfilling environments.

Key #8: Mental Sidestep

We are not always able to dictate and control circumstances. Often there are more variables that are outside our control than are in our control. However, we as individuals can always have control over ourselves and how we respond to particular circumstances and interactions with other people. We always have the ability to THINK.

When we take the time to think through all things, then we can practice a mental maneuver that I call a 'Mental Sidestep'.

Mental Sidestep - Recognizing unfavorable or adverse situations or interactions with people, and assessing the situation and your own feelings so that you can maintain your composure and react in ways that are non-detrimental and the overall best response at the time.

Key #9: Break Free From Your Prison

Getting Free. Freeing ourselves from all things that keep us falling short of glory . To be free from mental and spiritual hinderances that impede our positive growth & evolution, placing a block acting the doorway if our elevation. It's on us to get centered and come close to God and the God within us. Claiming God and being aware of ourselves and our true potential to accomplish anything that we impose our will on and apply ourselves to.

Life is constantly expanding; showing and proving the oneness of God and God's propensity and absolute nature to add on to life infinitely. Each of our individual thoughts themselves are suggestions for an add on to our reality. Once we move and turn that thought into action then there is immediate manifestation and creation. God expands the universe yet again.

Key #10: Ignorance Is Not Bliss: The Necessity Of Reading

NECESSITY - something that cannot be done without. A necessity is something that is absolutely needed. Reading, and reading often, is a necessity in striving to gain enlightenment. Constant reading is an absolute must in striving for intellectual and spiritual growth and development, especially in the 21st century where things are changing perpetually and becoming more sophisticated. When we read, we are able to acquire new information. With new information being stored in the great computer that is our minds, our thoughts change. Our thoughts dictate our actions, and it is thought and action that moves the universe and causes manifestation. Simply put, what we think and do ultimately dictates what we bring into the world and into our lives. I could not tell you to T.H.I.N.K. - Take-Heed-In-New-Knowledge without telling you to read. Reading is one of the best, and arguably the best, ways to acquire new knowledge. Ignorance is ungodly; almost every way of life and religion has a reference book, doctrine, or literature that can be read. Women and men throughout history have created literary works to record information and manifest ideas. So many literary works and writings have been made to serve as plates of spiritual and intellectual foods that we can ingest to nourish and enrich our mind and spirit.

So many devilish and unrighteous individuals and organizations have looked or look to keep people ignorant and unaware. A devil, being one who is moving in negative energies with the intent to lie, kill, steal, and destroy, uses ignorance as a tool to reach its goals. Therefore, we should look to destroy ignorance and disable the power of devils. It is difficult for a devil to bring ruin, deception, and death to an individual who is informed, aware, and thus protected from their unrighteous attacks and motives.

Inside books, there is a wealth of knowledge that can expand our minds and induce thoughts that propel us into actions that create abundance in the lives of ourselves and others. Within books, there are truths that can enlighten us and enrich our spirits so that we can gain peace of mind and grow & develop into better people. How can we take heed in new knowledge if we never seek the knowledge? How can we attain knowledge if we never put ourselves in contact with it? For the endeavors that you pursue in this world, you will need to gain as much knowledge about the associated aspects to be successful in those endeavors. To gain truths that perpetuate spiritual growth and development, you will need to read and take in the spiritual foods that are recorded in so many books and divine writings. Reading affords us the asset of knowing. Ignorance is simply 'not knowing,' and there is certainly no bliss in that.

Key#11: Divine Purpose

Every creation has been made with a purpose. Whether that purpose is good or bad, it exists. Every part has its place, even when we may not readily understand the purpose of particular creations or components. One definition of the word

cosmos is: "The universe considered as an orderly whole."

"Uni" (One) ----- "Verse" (Turn): UNIVERSE. One turn, all in order. All the creations therein have their place and purposes. Although the place and purpose of things may not be infinite and have a prescribed time, they still have a purpose.

With all the above ideas considered, it's good to recognize that people and entities in this world have a purpose. These purposes can be for good or bad, depending on perspective. Nonetheless, the creations have their place and were set in place to fulfill some function. It's crucial to understand that just because one person's or thing's purpose or position may seem small, it doesn't diminish its significance by default. Honeybees are small in size and simply produce honey and fly from flower to flower. As they move from flower to flower, collecting nectar to bring back to their hives, they inadvertently carry and distribute pollen, aiding in the fertilization of plants. This process is crucial for the reproduction of many fruit-bearing plants, crops, and trees, supporting biodiversity and providing the foundation for the interconnected web of life on Earth.

God may have blessed you more or less in life. However, being blessed more or less does not dictate your significance to the overall whole of things. Nonetheless, everyone must play their part accordingly. Just as team sports players have a position with essential functions, we also have purposes and functions that are integral to the grand scheme of things. You are important, and it's crucial that you find and walk in your purpose.

The consequence of not walking in your purpose is to distort or frustrate the overall process for others in this life, leading to an unfulfilling life or meeting an early physical death. This means not fulfilling something essential to helping someone or the world at large, failing to manifest some happening or circumstance. Consequently, you feel a void or unrest in your mind and spirit because you are not doing that 'something' you were created to do. Consequently, you die before you should have because you were NOT doing what you were created to do.

The Spirit Of Kings, Queens, And Soldiers: Proverbs 31:4-7: "Wine is not for kings, O Lemuel; Not for kings to drink, Nor any strong drink for princes, Lest they drink and forget what has been ordained, And infringe on the rights of the poor. Give strong drink to the hopeless And wine to the embittered. Let them drink and forget their poverty, And put their troubles out of mind. Speak up for the dumb, For the rights of all the unfortunate. Speak up, judge righteously, Champion the poor and the needy."

For those of us blessed to be in positions of Kings, Queens, and Soldiers in the Army of God, it is imperative to recognize your position and act accordingly. It's easy to become distracted or have your purpose and paths deviate by devices meant to do just that. If you are purposed to be a special vessel to do God's work, then you have to be vigilant and on duty. If you were meant to be the one in your family to save generations and bring your bloodline to wealth, power, and prestige, then you have to be vigilant and on duty. If you are a community leader or influencer intending to do good and be an asset and help to the community and people you influence, then you must be vigilant and on duty.

Vigilant: awake; staying watchful and alert to danger and trouble.

Duty: any action required by one's position or by moral or legal considerations, etc.

Stay vigilant and on duty! Stay awake, watchful, and alert to danger or trouble, and engage in any actions required by the position you've taken.

Kings & Queens are leaders of the highest esteem. A King or Queen has no business being drunken or drugged up, where they can't be vigilant and on duty or where they forget their duties and what to be vigilant for. Your position is high and comes with perks AND responsibilities; thus, you must be responsible.

"Do not accept the position of King or Queen and then complain about the heaviness of the crown."

- Zay Perry

If you are a warrior in spirit and especially a warrior or soldier for God, then you cannot be drunken or drugged up. How can you be vigilant or on duty then? There's pride in being a good soldier or mighty warrior. Don't let that pride be negated by distractions and negative devices that can turn into vices.

Leave the abuse of alcohol and drugs to those in lower positions. Let them drink and drug their problems away. Let them drink and drug to forget unwanted memories. Is God not enough? Are drinks and drugs mightier than the Power of God? Kings, Queens, and Soldiers devise solutions to their problems and take action. They accept the things they have no ability to influence or change. They don't allow unpleasant memories or thoughts to hurt them or negatively influence their lives. They create the mental fortitude and circumstances to never re-experience the unwanted. They help others to not experience the unwanted and get through what they themselves already experienced. They choose not to pick mental scabs and decide that what happened in their past will not have power over them today. Kings, Queens, and Soldiers make a conscious decision to choose happiness and cast off spirits of sadness and depression. They use any anger they feel as fuel to take positive action in life and do positive works. They stand for those less blessed, less intelligent, with less influence, and having limited resources. They use their strength to aid and assist the weaker. They bless others by way of their blessings and ordained purposes & positions, and in turn, they are blessed.

King, Queen, and Soldier: walk in your purpose. Stay vigilant and on duty.

Key#12: Get Active

From all toil, there is some gain, But idle chatter is pure loss." - Proverbs 16:23

A lot of meaningless talk doesn't bring any profit, and a lot of gossip will yield no reward. It's a must to do work if we want to see gains. It's a must to stay away from gossip to avoid the loss of precious and usable time. Not only does gossip waste your time, but it also causes a loss of mind by dulling it with low vibrational rhetoric that has no value.

There's always a time to rest. There's always a time to be still. However, God most often tells us to get active. Even 'Faith' without work is a dead thing. Always remember to take action perpetually, and you'll perpetually move more into blessings, meeting them halfway. God shows power and receives praise by way of demonstration. So, who are we to be lazy, idle, but looking to receive something?

A commute is movement, and our commute is from idleness to purposeful action; from poverty to prosperity; from faithless to faithful; from weak to

Divinely strengthened; from wandering to ordered steps; from chaos to peace; and from sidestepping hatred to walking directly into love.

We can't live off potential and stored energy alone. Often, we commend and exalt the potential and what 'could be' when the true glory comes from energy in motion, being kinetic, manifesting, bringing into fruition, and taking the actions that allow destiny to be fulfilled and open the doors to miracles to take place. Talk is cheap indeed, and getting active is Godly.

"Do not love sleep lest you be impoverished; keep your eyes open and you will have plenty of food." - Proverbs 20:13

Key#13: Fortification: Armoring the Mind, Shielding the Soul

"I was sitting by my Self. I was sitting by my Self, but I was not alone. I was reading. Someone came to me and asked, 'What are you doing?' I replied, 'I am eating and exercising."

-Zay Perry

I'll provide additional insights into the previous quote. Maybe it might be confusing to you that I said that I was sitting by my Self but not alone. Possibly, it is perplexing that I said I was reading and when someone asked what I was doing, I said I was "eating & exercising." So, I will give some clarification and understanding. I said that I was sitting by my Self. I had gone off to sit next to my Self. So, I was sitting closest to my Self, but I was not alone because energies or spirits are always present, though we can't see them here on the physical plane, but we can feel them, and they often interact with us. They do different things at different times.

We are spirit, and our intentions can vary. So, of course, other spirits, though they can't be seen by us, their intentions vary as well. They can just be around with no interest in us, or they can be present with interest in us. Just as people can be neutral, benevolent, or malevolent; so can the unseen spirits. Thus, we have to be aware that the feelings or thoughts that come to us may be influenced by some energy or spirit around us and that these thoughts or feelings may not have originated from inside our Self. We can be around people who are moving with energies or spirits attached to them that could be negative. Spirits of sight, confusion, depression, addiction, etc.

So, when we have thoughts or feelings influenced by these spirits, then we have to be aware enough to catch them and assess ourselves and determine if these thoughts or feelings are our own. We have to swiftly cast off negative feelings and thoughts that we determine are not our own. We also have to embrace divine and positive thoughts and feelings that come to us.

Looking back at the quote I started with, where I said, "I am eating and exercising." You may ask, "How could you be eating and exercising when you said that you were sitting alone and reading?" However, when I said that I was eating and exercising, I was meaning that I was eating knowledge and information by way of the content that I was reading. Also, when I said that I was exercising my mind through deep thought. We truly become what we consume, and that doesn't apply solely to the actual food we eat but also applies to information and content we choose to ingest.

The kind of media we consume and material we read is a major influence on our being; what we become and who we are. If we are constantly taking in low vibrational music, low vibrational visuals, and low vibrational reading material that has lots of negativity and no positive stimulations, then we ourselves will become negative and non-stimulated. On the flip side, if we are taking in media & reading material that has educational, spiritually stimulating, and positively influencing value in them, then we will be the product of those things we ingested into our mind and spirit.

We can grow our mind and spirit positively based on what 'eat' mentally & spiritually. This is not to say that we should refrain from fun and entertainment, but if we find low quality and negative material most entertaining and addictive, then maybe we need to evaluate our Self and determine why we cherish what is low quality, low vibrational, and negative.

Key#14: Choose Software Over An Avatar : Mind Vs Matter

An avatar is only a physical manifestation or representation of a continuous entity. It is only a housing for the energy to dwell and operate through. Our avatar, or physical body, is only a medium that is used for us to do work or deeds in the physical space. Our avatar is not our actual self. Our actual self is that voice we hear when we think to ourselves. Our actual self is that energy or spirit within the avatar.

Just as many of us have created a digital avatar to be the representation of our self on one or more platforms in the digital space. Whether it be Snapchat, Instagram, Facebook, or even a game. That avatar is not the actual software or algorithm that directs the motions of the digital avatar. The software is what is directing the avatar and events on a particular platform. The software is the thing of substance and depth that lives within the hardware, our different devices, and gaming consoles. However, that hardware and avatars that live within them cannot complete any tasks or perform any functions without the software directing it.

Therefore, we can always upgrade, update, and improve our software to be able to allow our devices, consoles, and avatars to perform better and optimally. So, we can create awesome looking avatars with really dope features and operate them on the most futuristic and sophisticated devices, but what will be most important is the software that powers them and dictates the animations and functions that are able to be done. You are limited by the level of sophistication of the software.

In the same way that the digital avatars are manifested in a digital space, we are manifested here in the physical space. Our physical bodies being the equivalent to the digital avatar. Just as our consciousness and spirit being the equivalent of computer software. If we find it important to keep our software up to date and have the most sophisticated software to power our digital avatars, then why would we not see it as the greatest importance to enhance our consciousness to be able to direct our bodies in this life?

In order for us to be able to avoid allowing ourselves to suffer calamity and being put in negative situations, it is imperative that we keep our consciousness updated. We can get those updates by downloading relevant information constantly that will allow us to be well-informed and perpetually aware of what's going on in our world so that we can navigate through the obstacles and shield ourselves from the things and people that mean to do us harm. We can keep our consciousness updated by staying closely in tune with the original energy that is us, that Divine Spirit. We can strengthen and expand our personal software, or consciousness, by way of the information we put into it and the tools that we use to construct it. The tools needed to construct a sophisticated and high-level consciousness are love, awareness, knowledge, wisdom, and understanding. What good is an aesthetically pleasing avatar that has limited software? What good is a nice physique wrapped in designer clothing but being operated by a weak and limited consciousness? The more our consciousness is expanded in positivity and awareness, then the more we are able to get out of this life. There will be more we can do for self. There will be more we can do for our family and friends. There will be more that we can positively add to the world at large. A sophisticated, well-structured, and expanded consciousness will allow us to protect ourselves in all dimensions, suffer less pain, help others, be better people, get more out of this life, and be free.

So let us not focus solely on our physical avatars; our body, which is only a representation of us that is temporary. Rather, let us work diligently at improving and structuring an elite personal software; our actual

being that is not temporary and lacking substance, but is deep and eternal.

Key#15: Purposeful Detachment

When you are in elevation, you must understand that elevation is sacrifice—sacrifice of time, energy, and caring for the needs of those not moving with you in your upward trajectory. You must be equipped to ascend the mountain and pack lightly. You need the proper tools and help, which include the proper knowledge, information, and people who genuinely aid you. Packing light means not trying to carry along issues, thought patterns, or poor habits, along with people who are not on the journey of purposeful elevation. With that said, it's essential to refrain from becoming intellectually or emotionally entangled with people who have chosen to stay at the bottom of the mountain, engaged in matters and problems specific to that place.

When striving for elevation and pursuing your purpose, sacrifices become an integral part of the journey. It's not just about leaving physical baggage behind but also shedding emotional and mental burdens. The weight of constantly tending to the needs, emotions, and concerns of others can anchor you, making the ascent towards your goals arduous. While supporting loved ones is crucial, navigating your path to success requires focus and dedication.

Understanding the significance of detachment is key. It's not about abandoning relationships or disregarding familial ties; rather, it's about establishing boundaries. Carrying the weight of others' problems and staying emotionally invested in their struggles can drain your energy and divert your focus from your objectives. This doesn't mean severing connections but rather finding a balance that allows you to thrive while still offering support without compromising your journey.

At times, the ascent to your destined peak may demand solitude. Not everyone will comprehend your aspirations, and not everyone will be ready to climb alongside you. Surrounding yourself with individuals who uplift and inspire is crucial. These are the people who understand the importance of growth and are aligned with the pursuit of their purpose. Collaborating and learning from like-minded individuals foster an environment of progress, propelling everyone forward toward their respective summits.

The distinction lies in recognizing the distinction between genuine support and being pulled down by the weight of others' choices. Empathy and compassion are noble traits, but ensuring your own progression is not selfish; it's essential. Elevation demands sacrifice, including the willingness to set boundaries, release emotional entanglements, and seek companionship that nurtures your growth. This process isn't just about reaching a peak; it's about aligning with your purpose and living a fulfilled life that radiates positivity and inspiration.

Key#16: Become Obsessed With The Power Of Giving

"One man gives generously and ends with more, Another stints on doing the right thing and incurs a loss.

A generous person enjoys prosperity, he who satisfies others shall himself be stated. He who withholds grain earns the curses of the people, But blessings are on the head of the one who dispenses it."

-Proverbs 11:24-26

God is love, and thus, love is the greatest power. Giving is a showing and a supreme example of love in action. More and more each day, people become obsessed with the power of positions, the power of money, and other variations of so-called power. However, one of the greatest powers is in giving. Therefore, when we become obsessed with giving, we demonstrate God in action. Not giving would be a suppression of God. Wouldn't it be evil and devilish to suppress God? Would it not be an honor and the greatest privilege to be used by the Most High God? When we practice giving, we are either being used by God or using our own free will to let God be manifest and seen here in the physical realm.

When we get active, we are doing work. When we get active in wielding the power of giving, then we are truly engaging in perpetuating love and therefore perpetuating God. When we do positive giving, we are positively doing God's work. So many men and women would be happy to see that you've done their work for them or willingly helped them complete their tasks. Do you think that God would be pleased by seeing you help him do his work? We can spread love, spread God, when we exercise the power of giving.

God rewards us for giving in a positive way. The rewards we heap upon ourselves by giving are preset by God's design of the universe and the universal laws that govern it. We automatically recompense the energy we put out. The karmic law of reaping what we sow is one of God's beautiful presets in his automation of his grand design.

Just as we'd do well to recognize the power in giving, we'd also do well to recognize that anyone can take hold of and execute the power of giving. Unlike the perceived power that must be acquired through working yourself into a certain position or trying to gain the power of money, the power of giving is an actual power and not just a perceived or temporary power. Not only that, we are not restricted by circumstances or mundane restrictions to use the power of giving because everyone can give; giving is not exclusively material in nature. Meaning, you can give in a way that doesn't require 'things'. You can give kind gestures, kind words, help those in need, share your gifts or talents to be a blessing to others, or even create in ways that bring value and substance to people's lives. With that said, every single person can move in the power of God by moving with the power of giving. Most certainly, the power of giving is a worthy and life-giving obsession.

Key #17 : No More Crying Over Spilled Kool-Aid: No More Making Holidays Of Nightmares

Kool-Aid in a plastic pitcher. The flavor is "Red." It may say 'Cherry' or 'Strawberry' on the actual Kool-Aid pack, but where I'm from, the universal meme for those flavors is simply 'Red.' Never heard of Cherry or Strawberry, so Red-flavored Kool-Aid in a plastic pitcher, ready to be poured into my cup. When I do pour it, the Kool-Aid is thick and almost syrup-like. When I mixed my Red-flavored Kool-Aid, I was certain to add a ridiculous and purposely excessive amount of sugar to bring it to its syrupy state. So, it's thicker than your favorite Instagram model and contains enough sugar to induce a diabetic coma.

Though my Red-flavored Kool-Aid is ice-cold, in its perfect sugary print, and ready to be consumed; I accidentally do the unthinkable: I spill some of my Red-flavored Kool-Aid on the floor and on my fresh white t-shirt that was completing one of my favorite outfits. Now I've stickied the floor, and worst of all, I've left an annoyingly conspicuous bright red stain on my white t-shirt, ruining my feeling of being super clean & photoshoot-ready; ruining my day.

This happened to me, and I never let it go. For weeks, months, and years later, I perpetually cried about the Kool-Aid I spilled some time ago. I let the thought of it keep me from putting on nice outfits. I stopped enjoying flavors outside of Kool-Aid. I stopped talking to people as much. I quit exercising and gained unhealthy weight. I would cry and not give anything any positive effort. When someone would sense that something was wrong with me, try to address the change in me, or tried to pry into what was ailing me, I'd think about that day I spilled the Kool-Aid and complain, weep, moan about it, and get down about how that Kool-Aid ruined my outfit on that day years ago.

Of course, if not sure from it happening, but I refused to let that miscue and unfortunate event go. I decided I'd never let it go and let it negatively impact me and keep all those same feelings of when it first happened stored securely in the back and forefront of my mind so I could readily reference it and cry and complain about it happening. I can't change that it happened, and it did not kill me, but I insist on letting it kill my spirit and cry about it perpetually.

Now, doesn't it sound ridiculous, unproductive, and utterly a waste of energy to dwell on and cry about some Kool-Aid I spilled in the past? I know that it most certainly does sound ridiculous and makes no sense to let that one unfortunate event subtly ruin my life. It DEFINITELY makes no sense to constantly cry and complain about something unfortunate that happened to me or a mistake or bad choice that I made. So whether the seemingly bad or unfortunate happened yesterday or 10 years ago, there's nothing productive about crying and complaining about something that has happened in the past that we certainly cannot change.

Life isn't always sunny days. Life also doesn't allow all things to go perfectly in our favor in every situation. Unfortunate events take place. Utterly terrible things can and may have happened to us for seemingly no reason at all. Bad things can happen to us. Bad situations can happen to us. Bad people can happen to us. Sometimes we heap those troubles on ourselves. Other times it's no doing of our own. No matter the varying circumstances in your life, there's no reason to harbor guilt. There's no reason to continually feel painfully responsible for a happening. There's no productivity or healing in choosing to harbor pain and resentment. These are all things that are sitting in your mind. You are the consciousness. You have control over the mind. You have the choice to exercise mental strength and to move on from past events. You get to make the choice to dwell on things. So, you can allow the past to destroy you, keep you complaining, keep you crying, keep you stagnant, make you weak — or you can show and prove your mental fortitude; strength of mind.

Our childhood may have had hurtful experiences; we may have been mistreated; we may have lacked love; we may have been wronged by a romantic partner; we may have been wronged by someone we considered a friend; we may have been abused; we may have been raped or molested; you may have made bad choices; we may have gone to prison; we may have lost a sense; we may have been diagnosed with an illness; we may have lost a fortune; or we may have had any number of experiences that we truly wish never happened but we cannot change it. Although, we can change how we deal with it. We can choose to be strong. We can choose to let it go. We can vow to not let it shape us or our mental health in a negative way. You have the choice, you only. My grandmother would often say, "Nothing from nothing leaves nothing." This meant you can never get anything from nothing or zero. It is exactly what it is, nothingness and a waste of energy, and there is nothing to be begotten from crying over spilled Kool-Aid.

Key #18 : Aligning Internal and External Realms: Manifesting a Divine Existence

"The Lord founded the Earth by wisdom; He established the heavens by understanding...." - Proverbs 3:19

Wisdom is the application of knowledge. It is the use of the proper knowledge that you have acquired. It is wasteful for an individual to possess the proper knowledge and not put it to use. The 'proper knowledge' is the 'correct information.' To have attained the correct information and then act contrarily as if you know not what is right is an attribute of evil. The proper knowledge is the truth, and only evil looks too readily to conceal the truth. Only evil looks to exterminate or quiet those who bring the truth. God is Love, and God and Love are all-powerful. We should look to take on the attributes of God, and God is fearless; we should not fear if we have faith in God's power. There is no fear attached to pure love. Thus, it is ungodly and an exhibition of cowardice to fear the repercussions of those who look to extinguish the flame in light of the truth. Understanding is discernment; it is seeing. Seeing as it actually is and not as it appears to be. And so to have understanding is to be free from and not subject to illusions. Understanding, to its highest degree, is pure love. If you are free from the illusions that you are separate from God, the source, then you will see that we are all in and of the same source. And thus, would you elect not to love God and all the other subsidiaries of God which are yourself and others? If you could see people as they are and not as they appear to be -- if you could discern and understand all that makes them; their experiences, hardships, pains, struggles, joys, and perspectives, would you not give them grace as you want to receive grace? Grace being an overlooking of your mistakes because of love. Grace being forgiveness based on love. Pure evil does exist, and the subsidiaries of it as well. However, so many of God's children have simply been tainted and led astray by the consumption of improper knowledge and illusions. They have internalized them and often have come to take pride in them to the point of defending improper knowledge and illusion with their very life. Also, so many of God's children are tainted and led astray by inviting and allowing unclean spirits and evil energy to live in them. Therefore, it is not them that are pure evil, though they have been subverted and perverted. Understanding this fact can allow us to use wisdom to avoid these people when it's best, disable these people when it's best, or give these people grace when it's best. We can only pray for the proper knowledge, wisdom, and understanding to know when to make the absolute best actions for inaction. Take on the attributes of the Most High God, and you will be able to found and build up your 'Earth'; your physical self and conditions, and they will be good. Take on the attributes of the Most High God, and you will be able to establish your 'heavens'; your mind and consciousness so that you can move through this life with the wisdom, understanding, and good energy that will allow you good karma, positive happenings & circumstances, avoidance of misfortune & calamity, and the enjoyment of more life and the things you established in your 'Earth.' To have fortitude is to have strength of mind. The state of your mind is of most importance. You do yourself and others a great service when you care for the state of your mind. To have a mind that is void of God, void of peace, and in the state of constant torment is to be in hell. To have a mind that's filled with God, calm with peace, and in a state of perpetual bliss is to be in heaven. When your mind is unsettled, you're confused about the truth, suffocated in darkness, and you are completely dissatisfied with the circumstances of your life; you will experience hell. Contrarily, when your mind is serene, you've perpetually rejected fallacies, your mind has been illuminated, and the circumstances of your life bring you joy and peace; you will experience heaven. Your mind is the absolute best part of yourself. Your mind is a sacred temple where you store the best of you. It is where you should go to have solitude for meditation, reflection, and introspection. All of your internal affairs should be sorted out within the temple. The Temple of the Mind should be kept as clean as possible and decluttered. Cleanliness, do not soil the temple that you feel.

Removal of clutter so that there is no useless junk stored there so that there will be space for only what is good and useful. There should be non-stop innovation of this sacred Temple to make it better and strengthen the structure and pillars. It's also essential to employ faith, truth, light, and the proper knowledge to be the security that protects your temple from being shaken, infiltrated, desecrated, or destroyed by poor foods, destructive ideas, and unclean spirits. It is in the temple of our mind where we go to privately commune with the Highest God. When the upkeep is maintained and strengthening the structure of the temple are constant, then you can put your internal affairs in order. Once your internal state is solidified and properly maintained then by nature and rule, the external affairs must eventually come into agreement. What you create in the mental and spiritual will align with and manifest in the physical world. Take care of your mind. It is God's gift to you. It is precious. It is your source of life and your greatest asset.

Key#19 : Walking in Faith: Unveiling God's Power

God opens hearts. God opens minds. God can and will open doors that no man can close. There are pains, afflictions, and filthy spirits that only God can heal, resolve, and dispel. For all the openings that God can create, you must position yourself to receive the blessing by moving with faith.

I say this to say that if you say that you know the power of God, then you should always be conducting yourself as if you know God's power. You cannot say that you pray for God to lead you through and deliver you from the wilderness and that you wholeheartedly know God's power can and will do just that, yet refuse to walk forward because of what may happen. To refuse to move forward in fear would be to show, in your actions, or rather, inaction, that you indeed have no faith.

To have faith actually is to say, "Things may not look the best right now, but I'ma walk. I'ma walk anyway because I have faith that God got me, no matter how it may look right now.

Why? Because : We walk by faith and not by sight alone. For we live by faith, not by sight." -2 Corinthians 5:7

How can you receive the blessing if you are out of position at the time that the blessing was supposed to come to you? People often like to say that they are playing the game of life, but life is not a game. When you lose on PlayStation, you can reset the game and 'run it back.' When you lose in spades, you can reshuffle the cards, redeal, and 'run it back.' You lose a pickup game in basketball; you can start a new game from zero and 'run it back.' But life doesn't work like that, and thus it is not a game. Though we can take a lesson from the game of basketball when we think about faith and our approach to life. Basketball is a game of positions and all about positioning. If you're not in the right spots at the right times, then you won't be successful in the game. You must box out to position yourself for rebounds. You have to get to your sweet spot to get the shots you want. You have to position yourself on defense to keep the opposing team from scoring. You must move around to get in the right spot to get the pass to score. So just like in basketball and its emphasis on positioning, we must move into the right spots and move accordingly to be able to receive the beautiful things that God has in store for us or to forge the fulfilling life of abundance that we desire to have.

It may be God's plan to give you the most life-changing blessing when you get to point 'D.' But because you lack faith and didn't truly believe in God's power, you stay at point 'A' or give up when things get difficult at point 'C.' When all you must do is walk, and blessings are right around the corner. It may look cloudy at point 'A,' but you walk, and when you get to point 'B,' there are some setbacks and obstacles, but God is there to see you through and allows you to stay the course. Then you arrive at point 'C,' and all kinds of things present themselves as huge hurdles. The devil gets active because he wants to rob you of the blessings that are to come. All kinds of evil spirits, demons, and negative energies they carry try to get active in your life because they want to distract you, tire you out with struggle, and make you lose faith and give up. It may seem like people, strangers, family members, and so-called friends start acting negatively in your life, but it's not always the people themselves, but those demons that have attached themselves to the individuals with the intent to use them as tools and devices against you. But you remember that scripture of the Bible did not say that the weapons would not form; it simply said that they would not prosper. Meaning, the weapons would not fulfill the task that they were sent to do in your life because God will show his children favor and grace, and thus the enemy will not have victory over you. You remember that and you walk. You sidestep, move around, and walk through the obstacles. You may have grown tired and weary, but you never lost faith in this you are rewarded and arrived at point 'D' where you finally received the life-altering blessings that God has laid up for you to allow you to accomplish what your heart desires because your heart was right, your spirit was like common, your intentions were good, and you showed and proved that you have faith by walking with it. Faith without works is a dead thing. *"In the same way, faith by itself, if it is not accompanied by action, is dead." -James 2:17*

Faith is the substance of things hoped for but unseen. It's the belief that it indeed shall be so though it may not seem that way right now. The works are the acting as if it is already so, or you are sure that it will happen because you have faith in God's power. The works are the walk. So, let's walk-- let's move, and do it all in strong faith.

Key#20 : Breaking Chains: Liberation from Harmful Patterns and Conduct

As spiritual entities, we navigate the experiences of human existence. As human beings, we can't become subject to various forms of vice. So many of us have or have had vices. These differences can feel so good to us that we don't recognize them as being a detriment or harmful to us. It's important to know and understand what a vice is and how it can restrict us from being most useful to God and keep us from elevating to the best person we can be.

Vice: (a) A morally bad, wrong, or wicked action. (b) Harmful or injurious conduct; conduct that causes harm or pain.

Morally bad, wrong, or wicked actions are not pleasing to God and will not lead to self-improvement. Harmful or injurious conduct; conduct that causes harm or pain is not pleasing to God and will not lead to self-improvement.

Some individuals might say that their former vices helped them become the person they are today, helped them learn valuable lessons, or you. That does not mean this is what God necessarily intended for you. However, God can use our missteps and the circumstances that we create for His purpose, which may be to bring you low so He can then bring you high by bringing you to Him.

Recognizing and overcoming vices is crucial on our spiritual journey. Today's world is rife with temptations that may seem pleasurable but can hinder our connection with God and impede personal growth. Avoiding morally wrong actions and harmful conduct is essential to maintaining a high vibration, strengthening the spirit, and staying close to God. While some may argue that past vices shaped them, it's vital to discern God's intended path, allowing missteps to become steppingstones toward divine elevation.

Key #21 : Rise Up : The Power Of Ascension

The power of your thoughts is profound, shaping the very fabric of your existence. In the pursuit of a fulfilling life, the keys provided in this transformative book underscore the pivotal role of cultivating a positive and empowered mindset. Emphasizing that the quality of your thoughts directly influences the overall quality of life, this book urges a departure from mediocre, low-value thinking. It contends that embracing a mindset aligned with growth, optimism, and purpose is paramount. In the crucible of thought transformation, this book posits that mediocrity begets dissatisfaction, urging readers to elevate their thinking to transcend a basic existence. Through this lens, this book illuminates the path to a more enriching and satisfying life, rooted in the transformative power of intentional, elevated thinking.

In the journey of life, ascending personally, financially, and spiritually holds profound significance. The 21st and final key in this transformative book is a call to rise up. Elevating yourself on these levels is not merely a pursuit of success but a holistic enhancement of life's quality.

Financial prosperity provides the means to manifest dreams and contribute positively to the world. Yet, the pinnacle lies in spiritual ascension and nurturing a deep connection with God. This spiritual foundation becomes the anchor, guiding you through challenges and triumphs, adding a profound richness to existence.

The culmination of the 21 keys underscores the vital importance of rising above mediocrity, embracing a life of substance and value. Internalizing each key becomes a shield against the mundane; a protection against the pull of a basic existence. These keys, when woven into the fabric of your mind, fortify your thinking against mediocrity; propelling you towards a life of purpose and fulfillment.

In the symphony of personal growth, keeping God first is the guiding melody. It not only provides strength in adversity but also aligns your journey with a higher purpose. As you rise up, you not only transform your own life but become a beacon of inspiration for others.

The call to rise up encapsulates the essence of a truly enriched life. It's a symphony composed of personal, financial, and spiritual notes; harmonizing to create a melody of significance and purpose. Shield your mind with these keys, protect your essence, and keep God first — therein lies the key to transcending the ordinary and embracing the extraordinary.

Rise out of any dark place. Rise out of making excuses not to do what your heart knows is right. Rise out of ignorance and become informed about many meaningful things, especially those things that won't increase the value you give to others as a person and increase your quality of life. Rise out of laziness because the sleeper will be impoverished. Rise out of hatred and let love live because over time love can heal. Rise out of being a victim and take a hold of victory. Rise out of strongholds of the spirit of depression. Rise out of unpleasant and hateful memories from an earlier part of your life. Rise out of not forgiving yourself for the mistakes you may have made because you are human. Rise out of blaming yourself and others for negative happenings. Rise out of mental and spiritual slavery. Rise out of the everyday mediocre, low value, and basic routines and do what will produce life, love, extraordinary inspiration, and a positive example that others can reference, and God can use to show his glory.

Remember that when you rise out, you don't know which part of the places you may find yourself as you move through your upward trajectory. However, your attention maybe infinite, and your life and legacy will be anything but mediocre, low value, and basic.

You have the keys—use them.

Made in the USA
Middletown, DE
02 July 2024

56683952R00042